First Sums
Activity Book

for ages 4-5

This CGP book is full of bright and colourful activities for children in Reception.

It's a brilliant way to introduce Addition and Subtraction — and it's stacks of fun too!

Helpful Hints

- A grown-up can help you read the questions. Let them know what you've been learning at school.

- Find a nice place to work. Make sure you're comfortable at your desk or table.

- Use a pencil to write or draw your answers. You can use coloured pencils to colour in the pictures.

- Work neatly, and try to keep your pencil inside the lines.

- Writing the numbers nice and clearly is really important — you can practise this on a separate piece of paper.

- The 'Snail Adventure' activity in the centre uses maths skills from the whole book — you may want to save this until last.

Published by CGP

ISBN: 978 1 78908 894 6

Editors: Hannah Lawson, David Ryan, Caley Simpson and Tamara Sinivassen

With thanks to Gail Renaud and Glenn Rogers for the proofreading.
With thanks to Emily Smith for the copyright research.

Printed by Elanders Ltd, Newcastle upon Tyne.
Graphics used on the cover and throughout the book © Educlips.
Cover design concept by emc design ltd.

Text, design, layout and original illustrations
© Coordination Group Publications Ltd. (CGP) 2022
All rights reserved.

Photocopying this book is not permitted, even if you have a CLA licence.
Extra copies are available from CGP with next day delivery • 0800 1712 712 • www.cgpbooks.co.uk

Contents

Adding On 1 or 2	2
Taking Away 1 or 2	4
Adding	6
Taking Away	8
Puzzle: Snail Adventure	10
More Adding	12
More Taking Away	14
Using Number Lines to Add	16
Using Number Lines to Take Away	18
Number Bonds to 10	20
Bubble Bingo	22

Adding On 1 or 2

How It Works

Count forwards to add on 1 or 2.

One more than 1 is 2.

Two more than 3 is 5.

Now Try These

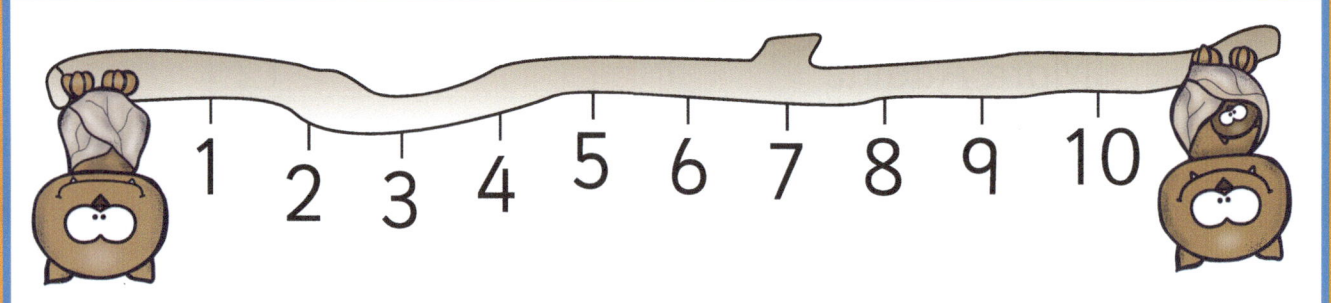

Colour in one more star. Then complete the sentence.

One more than 5 is **6**

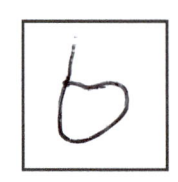

Find the number that is one more than the number shown. Write it in the box.

3 → One more → **4**

9 → One more → **10**

Count the stars. Then add two more to the bunting.

How many stars are there now? [6] stars

Find the numbers that are one more or two more than the number on the owl. Write each number in the correct box.

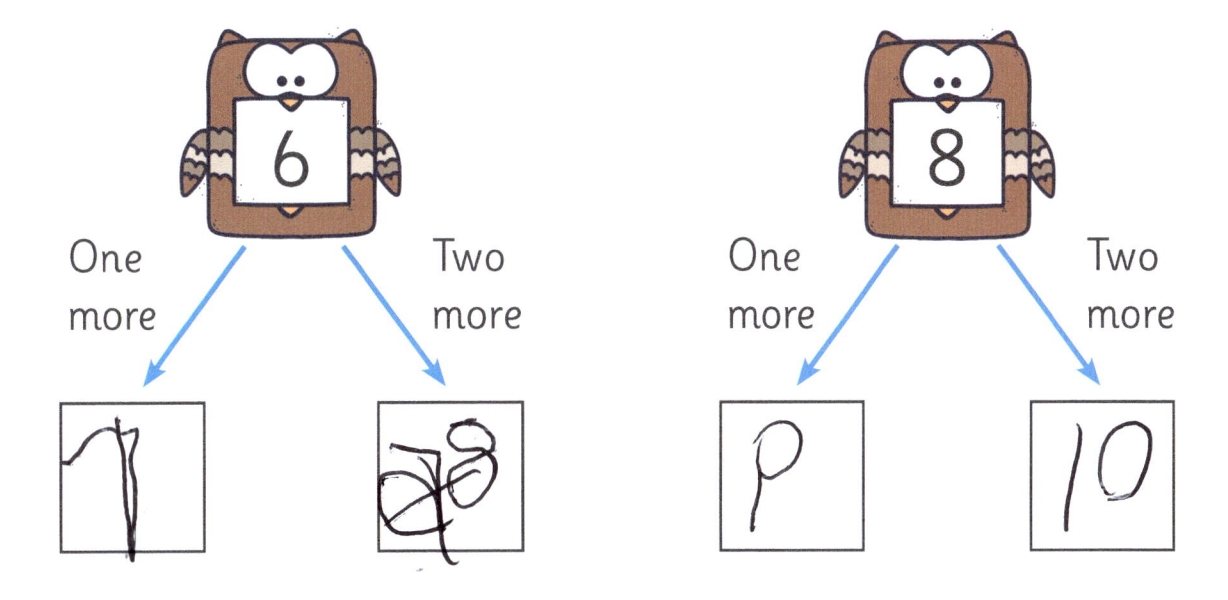

6 — One more: [7] — Two more: [8]

8 — One more: [9] — Two more: [10]

Circle the number that is two more than the number on the moon.

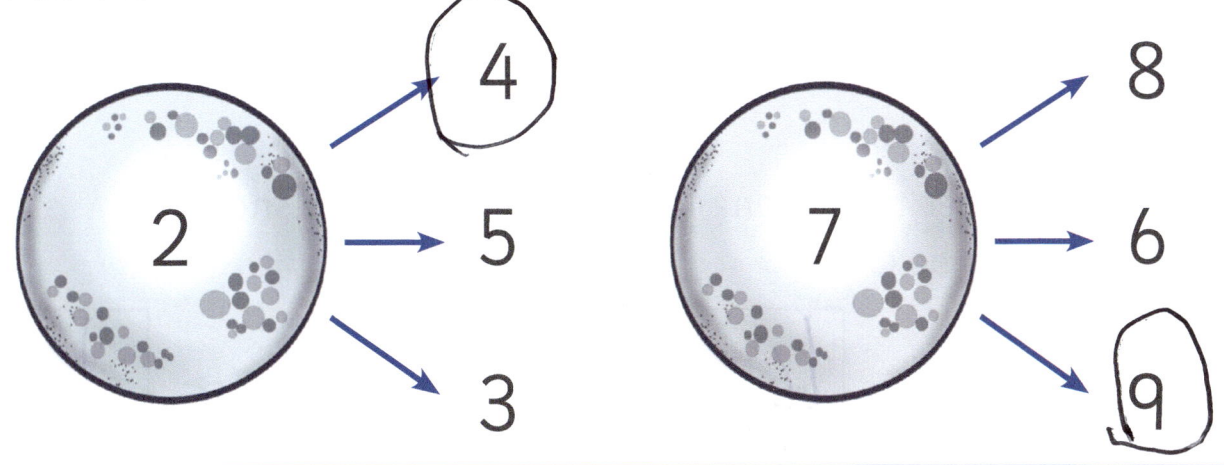

2 → (4), 5, 3

7 → 8, 6, (9)

Tick the box if you've learnt one or two more things.

Taking Away 1 or 2

How It Works

Count backwards to take away 1 or 2.

One less

1 2 3 4 5 6 7 8

Two less

One less than 3 is 2.

Two less than 8 is 6.

Now Try These

1 2 3 4 5 6 7 8 9 10

Complete each sentence by circling the correct raindrop.

One less than 8 is   6   ⑦   9

Two less than 10 is   ⑧   9   7

Find the number that is one less than the number shown. Write it in the box.

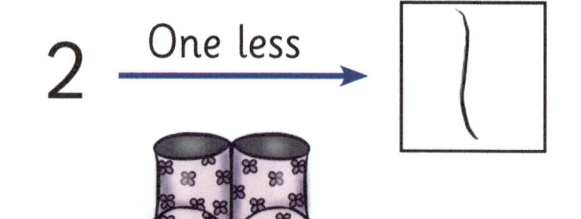

5 →One less→ 4

2 →One less→ 1

4

Count the welly boots. How many welly boots would Jake have on his shelves if he had two less? Write your answer in the box.

5 welly boots

Find the numbers that are one less or two less than the number shown. Write each one in the correct box.

6 — One less → 5
6 — Two less → 4

9 — One less → 8
9 — Two less → 7

Draw a line to match the number on the cloud to the number that is two less than it.

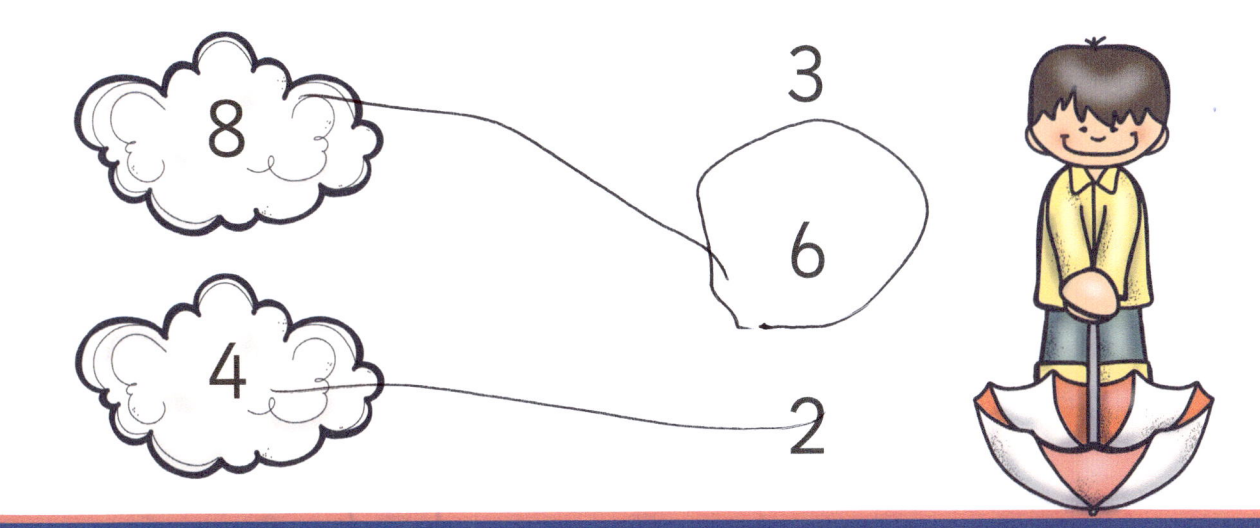

8   3
     6
4   2

Taken away some knowledge? Tick the box.

Adding

How It Works

Count the bicycles. Then add them together.

3 and 3 makes 6

Now Try These

Count the cars. Then add them together.

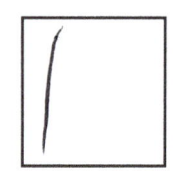

and   makes

1 and 2 makes 3

Add the planes. Circle the number.

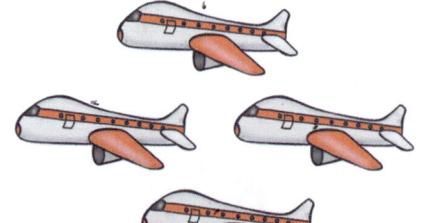

and 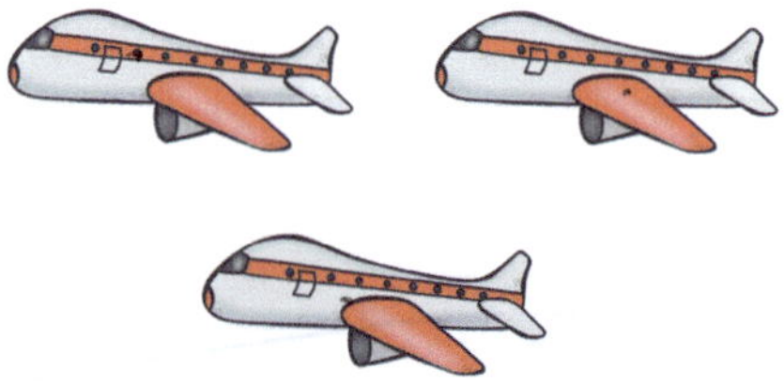 makes

1 2 3 4 5 6 ⑦ 8 9

Add up the wheels. Draw the answer.

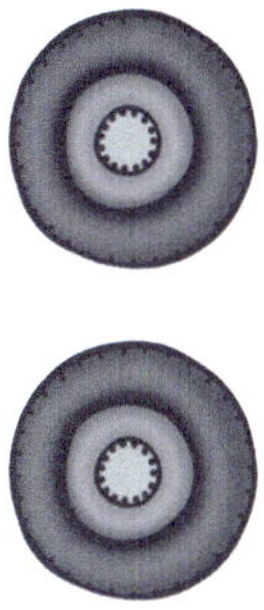

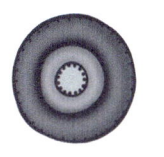

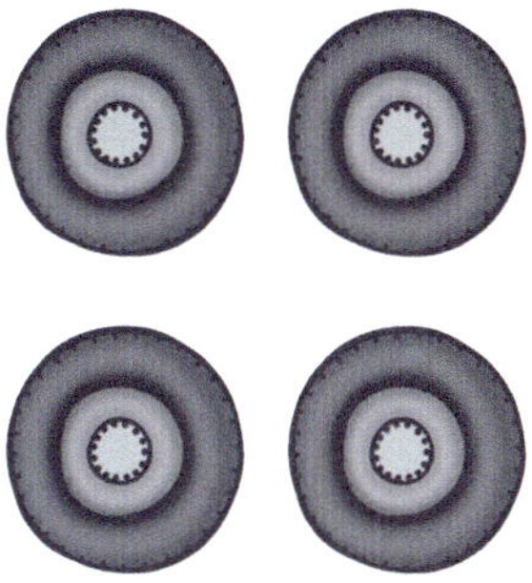

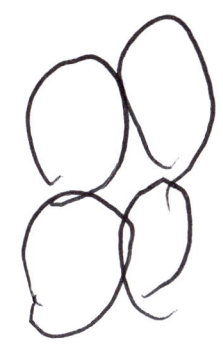

2   add   4   equals   6

How many of each vehicle are in the car park?
How many are there in total?

Number of cars: 2   Number of motorbikes: 3

Total number of vehicles:

5   add   3   equals   8

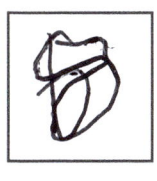

You're speeding ahead! Tick the box.

Taking Away

How It Works

Count the dragonflies. Then take one away.

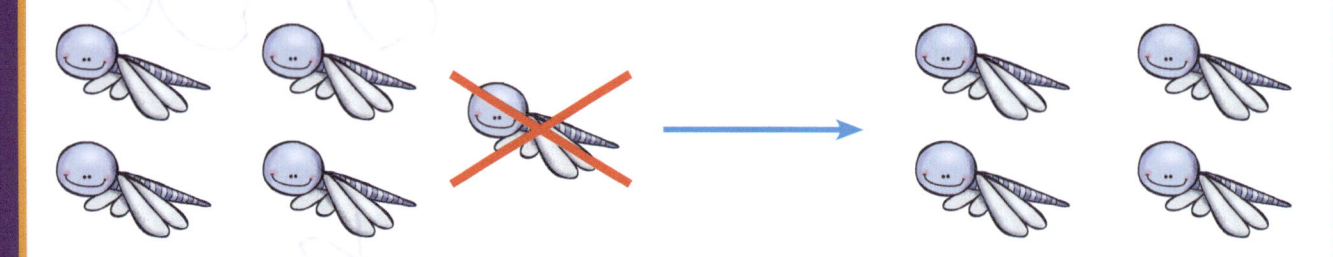

5 dragonflies

5 take away 1 is 4.

Now Try These

There are four frogs. Two hop away.
Colour in the number of frogs that are left.

Count the newts. Then fill in the boxes.

take away    is

6   take away   2   is   4

Count the flowers. Then take one away.

6 take away 1 equals 5

Count the fish. Then take three away.

8 take away 3 equals 5

Circle the 7 dragonflies ( ) flying around the pond.

Four fly away. How many are left?

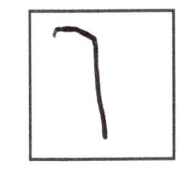

7 take away 4 equals 3

Great work! Tick the box.

Snail Adventure

3 snails set off on an adventure.
How many snails make it to the end of the path?

3 →

Use the boxes to keep track of the number of snails.

3 young snails get off the school bus. Add 3!

6 snails stop to play in a puddle. Take away 6.

10

4 snails join from a nearby farm. Add 4!

2 snails leave to go on holiday. Take away 2.

The end! How many snails are left?

More Adding

How It Works

Sums can show two numbers added together.
The **+** sign means 'add'. The **=** sign means 'equals'.

1 + 3 = 4

Now Try These

Add up the chillies.

2 + 5 = 7

Add up each group of pizza toppings.

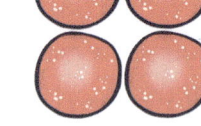

1 + 4 = 5

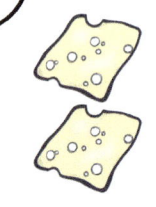

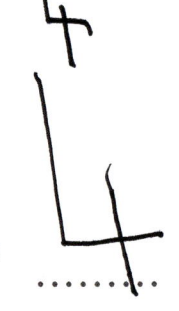

2 + 2 = 4

2 + 4 = 6

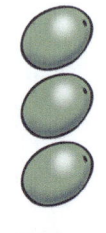

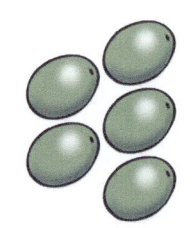

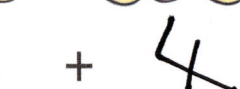

3 + 5 = 2

Aria is making a ham and pineapple pizza.

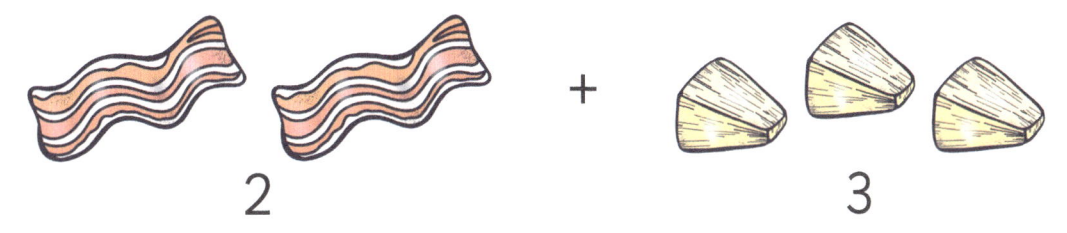

2 + 3

Add the number of toppings she uses. Circle the total.

1 2 3 4 5 6 7 8 9

Add the pizzas together.

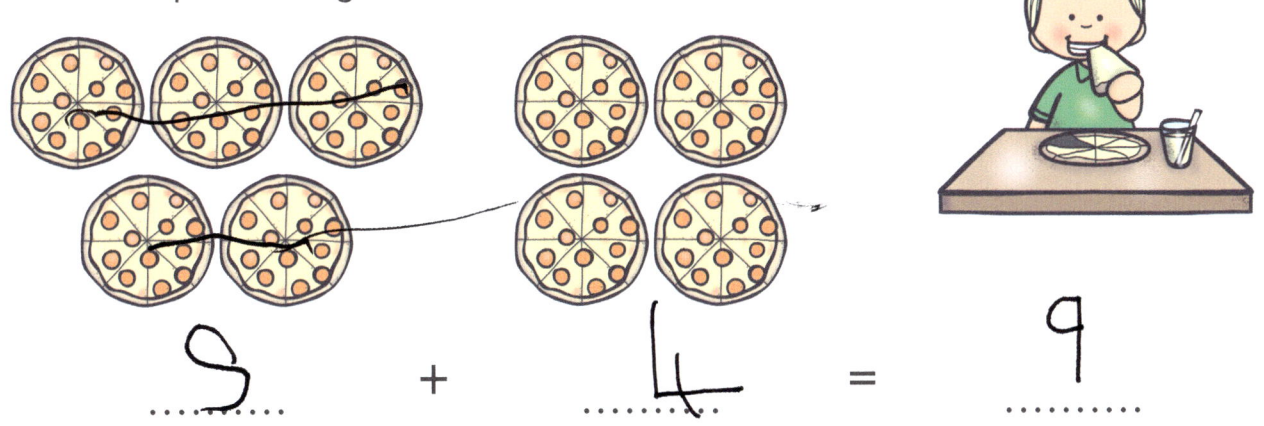

5 + 4 = 9

Find the answers to the sums. Circle the sum that shows the number of mushrooms on the pizza.

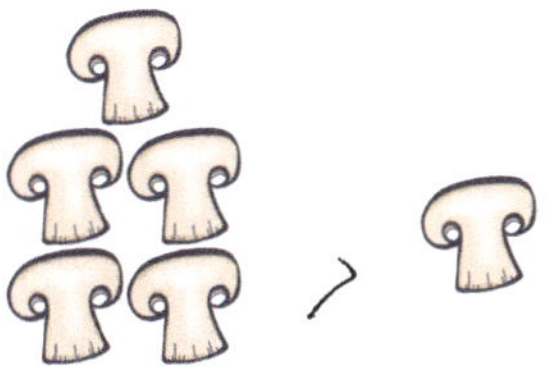

5 + 1 = 6   3 + 4 = 7

2 + 6 = 8

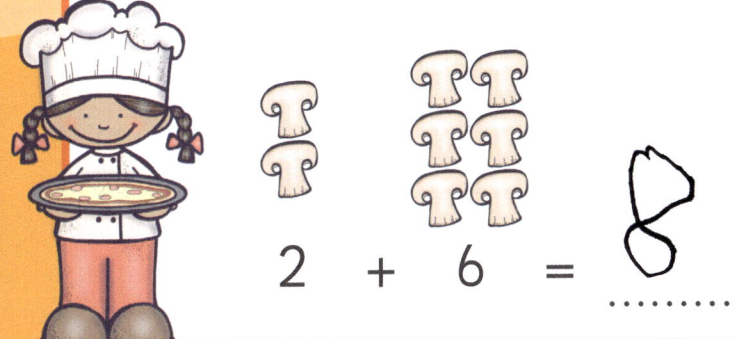

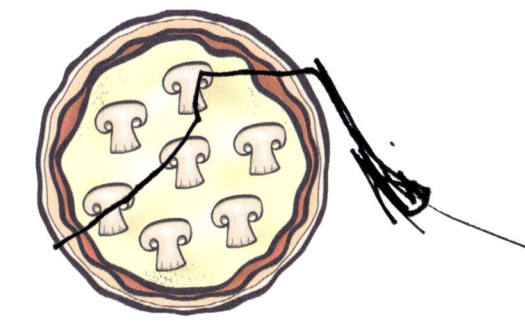

You're doing great! Tick the box.

More Taking Away

How It Works

Sums can also show one number being taken away from another number. The – sign means 'take away'.

4 – 2 = 2

Now Try These

Fill in the sum.

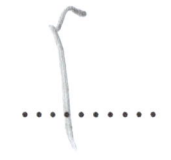

3 – 1 = 2

Work out how many treats are left after some are taken away.

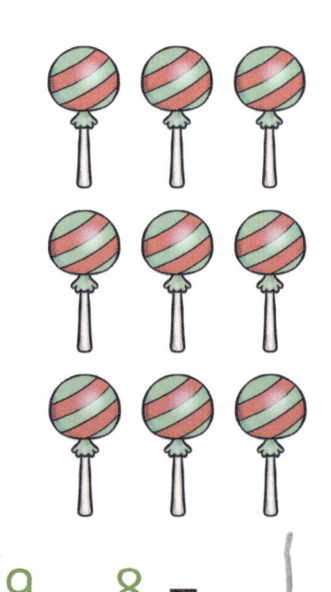

8 – 6 = 2   7 – 4 = 3   9 – 8 = 1

Arjun juggles 7 balls. He drops 3.

Circle the picture showing how many balls he has left.

7 − 3 =

A clown has 9 balloons. He gives away 4.
How many balloons are left? Fill in the sum.

....9...... − ....4..... = ...5......

Draw lines to match each sum to the right answer.

6 − 3

5 − 3

7 − 2

2

5

3

Fantastic job! Tick the box.

15

Using Number Lines to Add

How It Works

You can use number lines to add numbers.
Start at the first number and count forwards to add.

1 2 3 4 5 6 7 8 9 10

So 1 + 5 = 6

Now Try These

Add each pair of numbers. Circle the answer on each number line.

6 + 1

1 2 3 4 5 6 7 8

6 + 3

2 3 4 5 6 7 8 9

4 + 4

3 4 5 6 7 8 9 10

Ella folds 1 jumper. Her sister folds 3 jumpers.
Colour in the total number of jumpers they fold.

| 1 | 2 | 3 | 4 | 5 | 6 | 7 | 8 | 9 | 10 |

Use the number line to find the answers to the sums.

1 2 3 4 5 6 7 8 9 10

6 + 4 = ………   7 + 2 = ………

Tom has forgotten which washing machine he used.
The number on the washing machine Tom used equals 2 + 3.
Circle the washing machine that Tom used.

Keep up the good work! Tick the box.

17

Using Number Lines to Take Away

How It Works

Number lines can help you take one number away from another. Start at the first number and count backwards to take away.

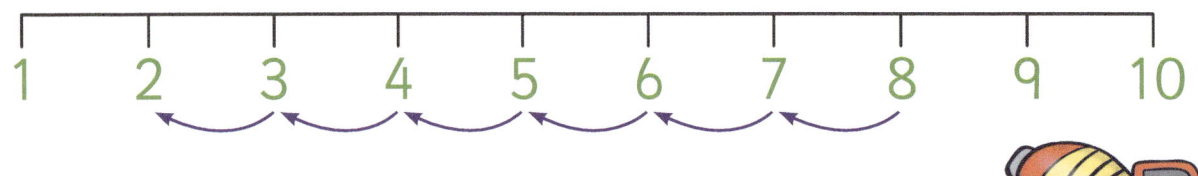

1 2 3 4 5 6 7 8 9 10

So 8 − 6 = 2

Now Try These

Amir has 9 screws in his toolbox. He uses 5.
Colour in the number of screws he has left.

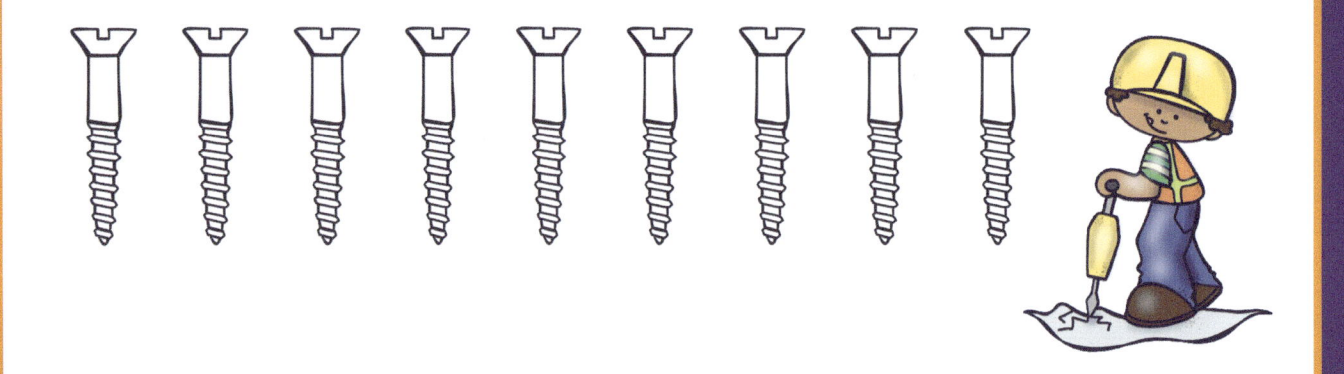

1 2 3 4 5 6 7 8 9 10

There are 5 piles of dirt. A digger clears away 2 of the piles. How many piles are left?

5 − 2 = ☐

Use the number line to find the answer to each sum.

2 3 4 5 6 7 8 9

7 − 5 = ☐   6 − 2 = ☐

Match each sum to the group with the correct number of objects. Use the number line to help you.

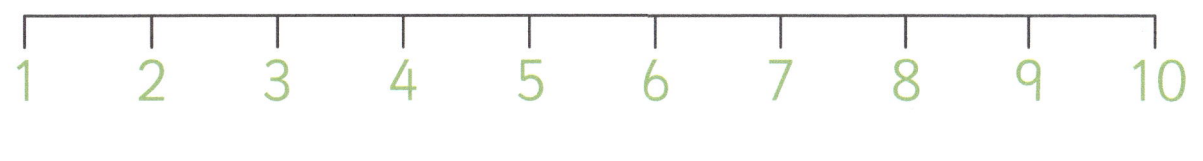

1 2 3 4 5 6 7 8 9 10

5 − 1   8 − 3   6 − 4

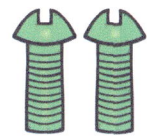

Tessa has a job at a house. The house number is equal to 9 − 3. Circle the house she needs to go to.

4 5 6 7 8 9

You're doing really well! Tick the box.

Number Bonds to 10

How It Works

These are the number pairs that add up to 10.

10 + 0 = 10   8 + 2 = 10   6 + 4 = 10

9 + 1 = 10   7 + 3 = 10   5 + 5 = 10

Now Try These

Match each hat to a snowman so that the numbers add up to 10.

Hats: 9, 2, 5, 10, 4

Snowmen: 8, 1, 6, 5, 0

Asmita likes to have 10 marshmallows in her hot chocolate. Circle the number of marshmallows she needs to add.

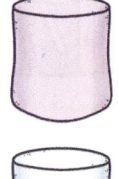

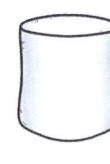

3

There are 5 baubles on the tree. Colour in the number of extra baubles needed for there to be 10 baubles on the tree.

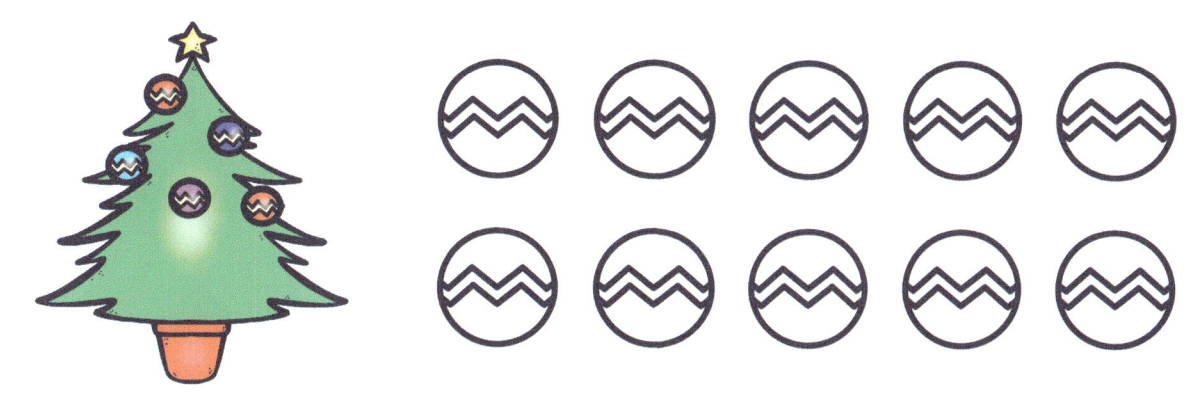

Each snowman is trying to make 10 snowballs.
Write how many more snowballs they each need in the boxes.

Each sleigh can fit a total of 10 presents.
The number on each sleigh shows how many presents are in it.
Match each sleigh to the stack of presents needed to fill it.

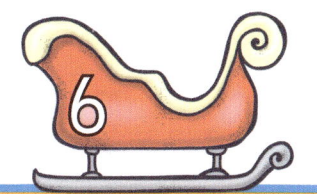

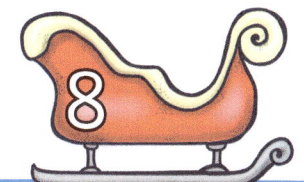

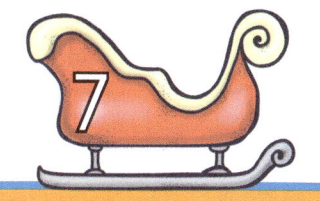

Amazing work! Tick the box.

21

Bubble Bingo

Pop the bubbles that show the answers to the questions below. One bubble will be left over.

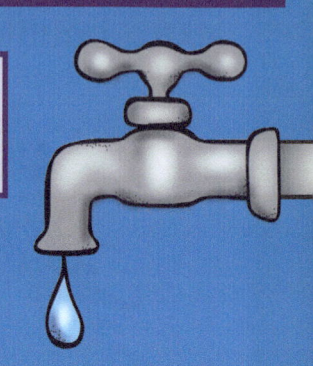

Pop the bubble that is one more than 3.

Pop the bubble that is two less than 8.

Pop the bubble that is the answer to **10 − 3**.

Pop the bubble that is the answer to **5 + 4**.

Pop the bubble that is one less than the number of ducks on this page.

Hint: cross out the bubbles as you pop them!

9   4   2

3   7   6

Which bubble has not been popped?